GW01255339

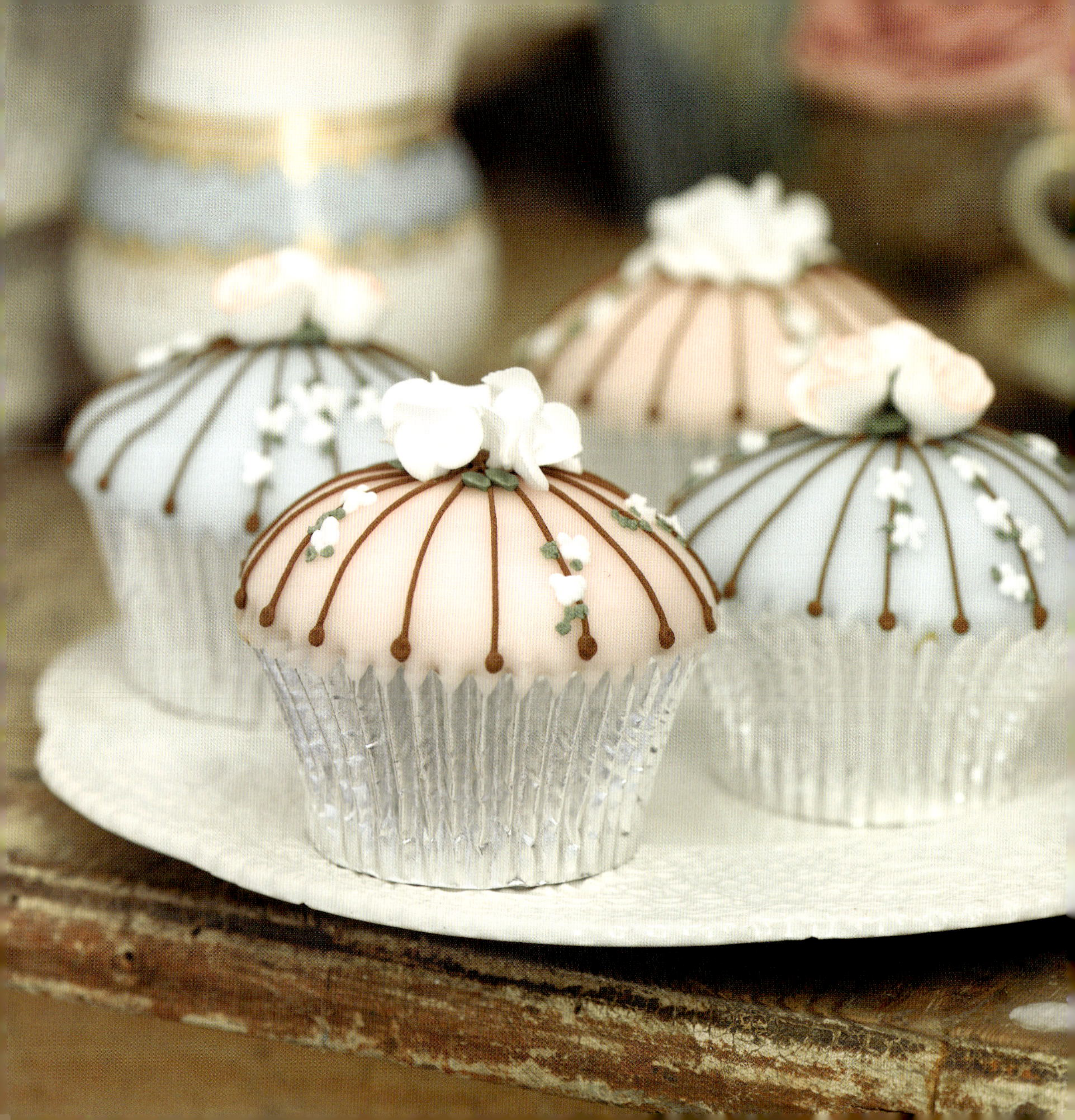

bake me I'm yours... cupcake

Diary 2012

D&C
David and Charles
www.bakeme.com

December–January

Monday 26th

Tuesday 27th

Wednesday 28th

December–January

Saturday 31st
New Year's Eve

Thursday 29th

Sunday 1st
New Year's Day

Friday 30th

January 2012

m	t	w	t	f	s	s
26	27	28	29	30	31	1
2	3	4	5	6	7	8
9	10	11	12	13	14	15
16	17	18	19	20	21	22
23	24	25	26	27	28	29
30	31	1	2	3	4	5

January

Monday 2nd
New Year's Day Holiday

Tuesday 3rd

January

Wednesday 4th

Saturday 7th

Thursday 5th

Sunday 8th

Friday 6th

January 2012

m	t	w	t	f	s	s
26	27	28	29	30	31	1
2	3	4	5	6	7	8
9	10	11	12	13	14	15
16	17	18	19	20	21	22
23	24	25	26	27	28	29
30	31	1	2	3	4	5

January

Monday 9th

Tuesday 10th

Lemon polenta — Makes 20 cupcakes

you will need
- 3 large eggs
- 200g/7oz caster (superfine) sugar
- 5 tbsp/75ml natural yoghurt
- 5 tbsp/75ml sunflower oil
- grated zest and juice of two lemons
- 175g/6oz polenta
- 50g/1¾oz plain (all-purpose) or gluten-free flour
- 1½ tsp/7.5ml baking powder

1 Preheat the oven to 170°C/325°F/Gas 3.

2 Line the cupcake tins with cupcake cases.

3 In a mixing bowl, beat the eggs and sugar until pale and creamy.

4 In a separate bowl, stir in the yoghurt, oil, lemon rind and 2 tbsp/30ml of lemon juice (reserve the remaining lemon juice for the syrup) until combined.

5 Add the yoghurt mixture into the eggs and sugar, beating continuously with a wooden spoon until smooth.

6 Sift the polenta, flour and baking powder into the batter.

7 Using a jug, pour the mixture (which is fairly runny) into the paper cases. They should be about three quarters full.

8 Bake for 20 minutes, or until a skewer inserted into the centre of one of the cupcakes comes out clean.

9 Allow to cool in the tray for 5 minutes before removing to a wire rack to cool completely.

January

Wednesday 11th

Thursday 12th

Friday 13th

Saturday 14th

Sunday 15th

January 2012

m	t	w	t	f	s	s
26	27	28	29	30	31	1
2	3	4	5	6	7	8
9	10	11	12	13	14	15
16	17	18	19	20	21	22
23	24	25	26	27	28	29
30	31	1	2	3	4	5

January

Monday 16th
Martin Luther King Day (USA)

Tuesday 17th

January

Wednesday 18th

Thursday 19th

Friday 20th

Saturday 21st

Sunday 22nd

January 2012

m	t	w	t	f	s	s
26	27	28	29	30	31	1
2	3	4	5	6	7	8
9	10	11	12	13	14	15
16	17	18	19	20	21	22
23	24	25	26	27	28	29
30	31	1	2	3	4	5

January

Monday 23rd

Tuesday 24th

Wednesday 25th
Robert Burns Night

January

Saturday 28th

Thursday 26th

Sunday 29th

Friday 27th

January 2012						
m	t	w	t	f	s	s
26	27	28	29	30	31	1
2	3	4	5	6	7	8
9	10	11	12	13	14	15
16	17	18	19	20	21	22
23	24	25	26	27	28	29
30	31	1	2	3	4	5

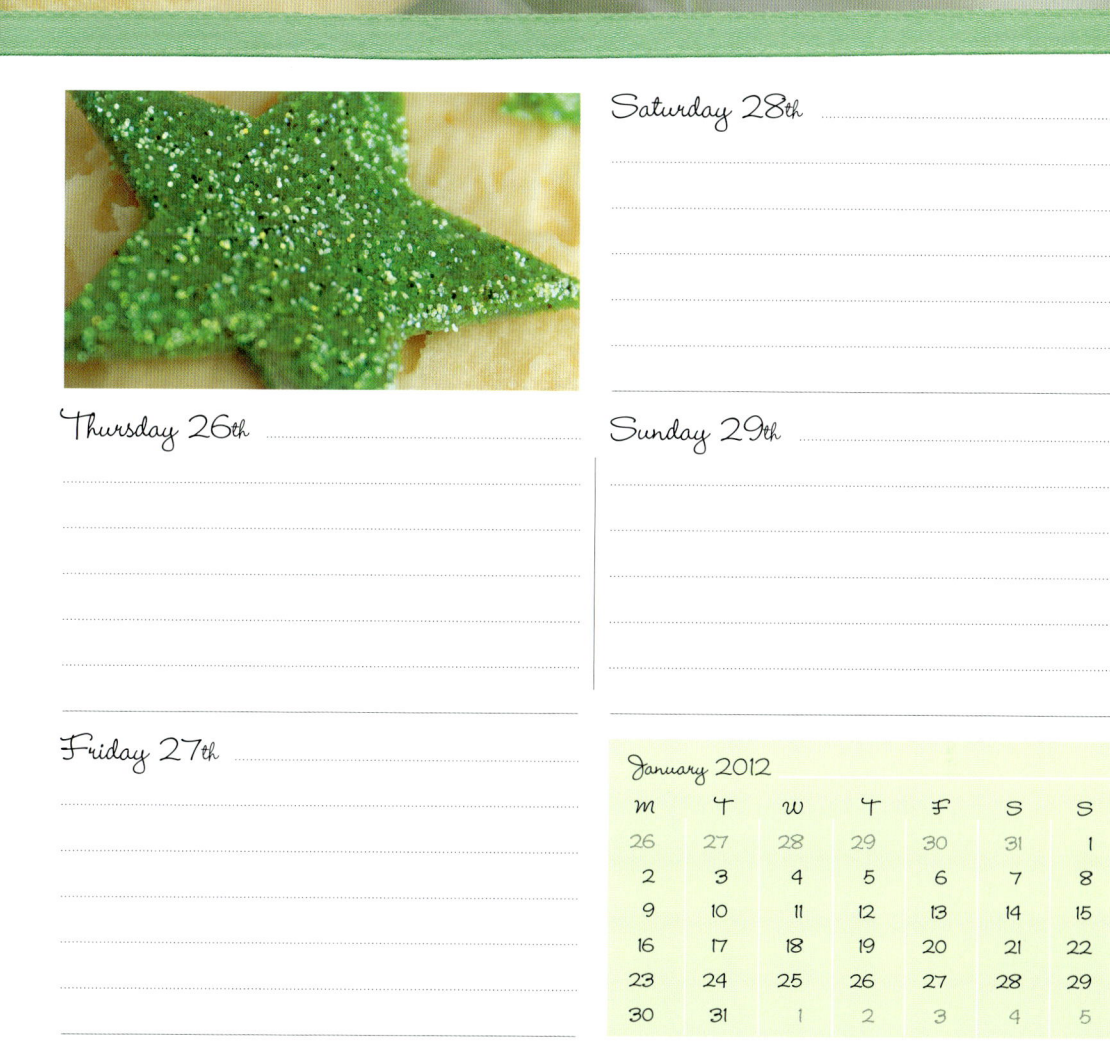

January–February

Monday 30th

Tuesday 31st

January–February

Wednesday 1st

Saturday 4th

Thursday 2nd

Groundhog Day (USA)

Sunday 5th

Friday 3rd

February 2012

m	t	w	t	f	s	s
30	31	1	2	3	4	5
6	7	8	9	10	11	12
13	14	15	16	17	18	19
20	21	22	23	24	25	26
27	28	29	1	2	3	4
5	6	7	8	9	10	11

February

Monday 6th

Tuesday 7th

Chocolate temptation
Makes 12 cupcakes

you will need

- 100g/3½oz slightly salted butter, softened
- 220g/7¾oz light brown sugar
- 1 tsp/5ml vanilla extract
- 2 medium eggs
- 160g/5¾oz self-raising (self-rising) flour, sifted
- 40g/1½oz cocoa powder (unsweetened cocoa), sifted
- 125ml/4 fl oz milk

1 Preheat the oven to 170°C/325°F/Gas 3.

2 Line the cupcake tin with cupcake cases.

3 In a large electric mixer, beat the butter and sugar together with the vanilla extract and the eggs until combined.

4 Add the dry ingredients and mix together on a slow speed while adding the milk. Make sure that all the ingredients are mixed together well.

5 Evenly spoon or pipe the mixture into the cases.

6 Bake in the oven for approximately 20 minutes or until a skewer inserted into the centre of one of the cupcakes comes out clean.

7 Brush the cakes with syrup and allow to cool in the tin for 10 minutes before removing to a wire rack to cool completely.

February

Wednesday 8th

Thursday 9th

Friday 10th

Saturday 11th

Sunday 12th

February 2012

m	t	w	t	f	s	s
30	31	1	2	3	4	5
6	7	8	9	10	11	12
13	14	15	16	17	18	19
20	21	22	23	24	25	26
27	28	29	1	2	3	4
5	6	7	8	9	10	11

February

Monday 13th

Tuesday 14th
Valentines Day

Wednesday 15th

February

Saturday 18th

Thursday 16th

Sunday 19th

Friday 17th

February 2012						
M	T	W	T	F	S	S
30	31	1	2	3	4	5
6	7	8	9	10	11	12
13	14	15	16	17	18	19
20	21	22	23	24	25	26
27	28	29	1	2	3	4
5	6	7	8	9	10	11

February

Monday 20th
Presidents' Day (USA)

Tuesday 21st
Shrove Tuesday (Pancake Day)

February

Wednesday 22nd
Ash Wednesday

Thursday 23rd

Friday 24th

Saturday 25th

Sunday 26th

February 2012

M	T	W	T	F	S	S
30	31	1	2	3	4	5
6	7	8	9	10	11	12
13	14	15	16	17	18	19
20	21	22	23	24	25	26
27	28	29	1	2	3	4
5	6	7	8	9	10	11

February–March

Monday 27th

Tuesday 28th

Wednesday 29th

Thursday 1st
St David's Day

Friday 2nd

February–March

Saturday 3rd

Sunday 4th

February 2012						
M	T	W	T	F	S	S
30	31	1	2	3	4	5
6	7	8	9	10	11	12
13	14	15	16	17	18	19
20	21	22	23	24	25	26
27	28	29	1	2	3	4
5	6	7	8	9	10	11

March

Monday 5th

Tuesday 6th

March

Wednesday 7th

Thursday 8th

Friday 9th

Saturday 10th

Sunday 11th

March 2012

m	t	w	t	f	s	s
27	28	29	1	2	3	4
5	6	7	8	9	10	11
12	13	14	15	16	17	18
19	20	21	22	23	24	25
26	27	28	29	30	31	1
2	3	4	5	6	7	8

March

Monday 12th

Tuesday 13th

Sugar syrup
Makes enough to soak 12 cupcakes

you will need
- 75ml/2½ fl oz water
- 75g/2¾oz caster (superfine) sugar

flavour variations
- **vanilla** add 1 tsp/5ml vanilla extract
- **citrus** replace the water with freshly squeezed, finely strained lemon, orange or lime juice
- **liqueurs** limoncello, Grand Marnier, Tia Maria or Malibu can also be added to enhance the syrup's flavour

1 Put the water and sugar into a saucepan and bring to the boil, stirring once or twice.

2 Add any flavouring and allow to cool.

3 Store in an airtight container in the refrigerator for up to one month.

Sugar syrup is brushed on to the cupcakes to add moisture and flavour. Ideally, this should be done while the cupcakes are still warm, to help the syrup soak further into the cakes. The amount of syrup used is a personal choice – if you feel that your cake is quite dry, use more syrup. However, be aware that by adding too much syrup your cake can become too sweet and sticky.

March

Wednesday 14th

Thursday 15th

Friday 16th

Saturday 17th
St Patrick's Day

Sunday 18th
Mother's Day (UK)

March 2012

M	T	W	T	F	S	S
27	28	29	1	2	3	4
5	6	7	8	9	10	11
12	13	14	15	16	17	18
19	20	21	22	23	24	25
26	27	28	29	30	31	1
2	3	4	5	6	7	8

March

Monday 19th

Tuesday 20th

March

Wednesday 21st

Saturday 24th

Thursday 22nd

Sunday 25th
British Summertime (BST) begins

Friday 23rd

March 2012

m	t	w	t	f	s	s
27	28	29	1	2	3	4
5	6	7	8	9	10	11
12	13	14	15	16	17	18
19	20	21	22	23	24	25
26	27	28	29	30	31	1
2	3	4	5	6	7	8

March–April

Monday 26th

Tuesday 27th

Wednesday 28th

March–April

Thursday 29th

Friday 30th

Saturday 31st

Sunday 1st
April Fools Day
Palm Sunday

March 2012

m	t	w	t	f	s	s
27	28	29	1	2	3	4
5	6	7	8	9	10	11
12	13	14	15	16	17	18
19	20	21	22	23	24	25
26	27	28	29	30	31	1
2	3	4	5	6	7	8

April

Monday 2nd

Tuesday 3rd

Wednesday 4th

April

Thursday 5th

Friday 6th
Good Friday

Saturday 7th

Sunday 8th
Easter Sunday

April 2012

m	t	w	t	f	s	s
26	27	28	29	30	31	1
2	3	4	5	6	7	8
9	10	11	12	13	14	15
16	17	18	19	20	21	22
23	24	25	26	27	28	29
30	1	2	3	4	5	6

April

Monday 9th
Easter Monday

Tuesday 10th

April

Wednesday 11th

Thursday 12th

Friday 13th

Saturday 14th

Sunday 15th

M	T	W	T	F	S	S
April 2012						
26	27	28	29	30	31	1
2	3	4	5	6	7	8
9	10	11	12	13	14	15
16	17	18	19	20	21	22
23	24	25	26	27	28	29
30	1	2	3	4	5	6

April

Monday 16th

Tuesday 17th

April

Wednesday 18th

Thursday 19th

Friday 20th

Saturday 21st

Sunday 22nd

April 2012

M	T	W	T	F	S	S
26	27	28	29	30	31	1
2	3	4	5	6	7	8
9	10	11	12	13	14	15
16	17	18	19	20	21	22
23	24	25	26	27	28	29
30	1	2	3	4	5	6

April

Monday 23rd
St George's Day

Tuesday 24th

Wednesday 25th

April

Saturday 28th

Thursday 26th

Sunday 29th

Friday 27th

April 2012

m	t	w	t	f	s	s
26	27	28	29	30	31	1
2	3	4	5	6	7	8
9	10	11	12	13	14	15
16	17	18	19	20	21	22
23	24	25	26	27	28	29
30	1	2	3	4	5	6

April–May

Monday 30th

Tuesday 1st

Wednesday 2nd

April–May

Saturday 5th
Cinco de Mayo (USA)

Thursday 3rd

Sunday 6th

Friday 4th

May 2012

m	t	w	t	f	s	s
30	1	2	3	4	5	6
7	8	9	10	11	12	13
14	15	16	17	18	19	20
21	22	23	24	25	26	27
28	29	30	31	1	2	3
4	5	6	7	8	9	10

May

Monday 7th
Early May Bank Holiday (May Day)

Tuesday 8th

Classic sponge — Makes 12 cupcakes

you will need

- 150g/5½oz unsalted (sweet) butter, softened
- 150g/5½oz caster (superfine) sugar
- ½ tsp/2.5ml vanilla extract
- 3 medium eggs
- 150g/5½oz self-raising (self-rising) flour

1 Preheat the oven to 170°C/325°F/Gas 3.

2 Line the cupcake tin with cupcake cases.

3 In a large electric mixer, beat the butter and sugar together with the vanilla extract until the mixture becomes light and fluffy.

4 Add the eggs gradually, beating well between each addition.

5 Sift the flour, add to the mixture and mix carefully until just combined.

6 Remove the mixing bowl from the mixer and fold the mixture gently through with a spatula. Evenly spoon or pipe the mixture into the cases.

7 Bake the cupcakes in the oven for approximately 20 minutes or until a skewer inserted into the centre of one of the cupcakes comes out clean.

8 Brush the cakes with syrup and allow to cool in the tin for 10 minutes before removing to a wire rack to cool completely.

May

Wednesday 9th

Thursday 10th

Friday 11th

Saturday 12th

Sunday 13th
Mother's Day (USA)

May 2012						
m	t	w	t	f	s	s
30	1	2	3	4	5	6
7	8	9	10	11	12	13
14	15	16	17	18	19	20
21	22	23	24	25	26	27
28	29	30	31	1	2	3
4	5	6	7	8	9	10

May

Monday 14th

Tuesday 15th

May

Wednesday 16th

Thursday 17th

Friday 18th

Saturday 19th

Sunday 20th

May 2012

m	t	w	t	f	s	s
30	1	2	3	4	5	6
7	8	9	10	11	12	13
14	15	16	17	18	19	20
21	22	23	24	25	26	27
28	29	30	31	1	2	3
4	5	6	7	8	9	10

May

Monday 21st

Tuesday 22nd

May

Wednesday 23rd

Thursday 24th

Friday 25th

Saturday 26th

Sunday 27th

May 2012

m	t	w	t	f	s	s
30	1	2	3	4	5	6
7	8	9	10	11	12	13
14	15	16	17	18	19	20
21	22	23	24	25	26	27
28	29	30	31	1	2	3
4	5	6	7	8	9	10

May–June

Monday 28th
Memorial Day (USA)

Tuesday 29th

May–June

Wednesday 30th

Thursday 31st

Friday 1st

Saturday 2nd

Sunday 3rd

May 2012

M	T	W	T	F	S	S
30	1	2	3	4	5	6
7	8	9	10	11	12	13
14	15	16	17	18	19	20
21	22	23	24	25	26	27
28	29	30	31	1	2	3
4	5	6	7	8	9	10

June

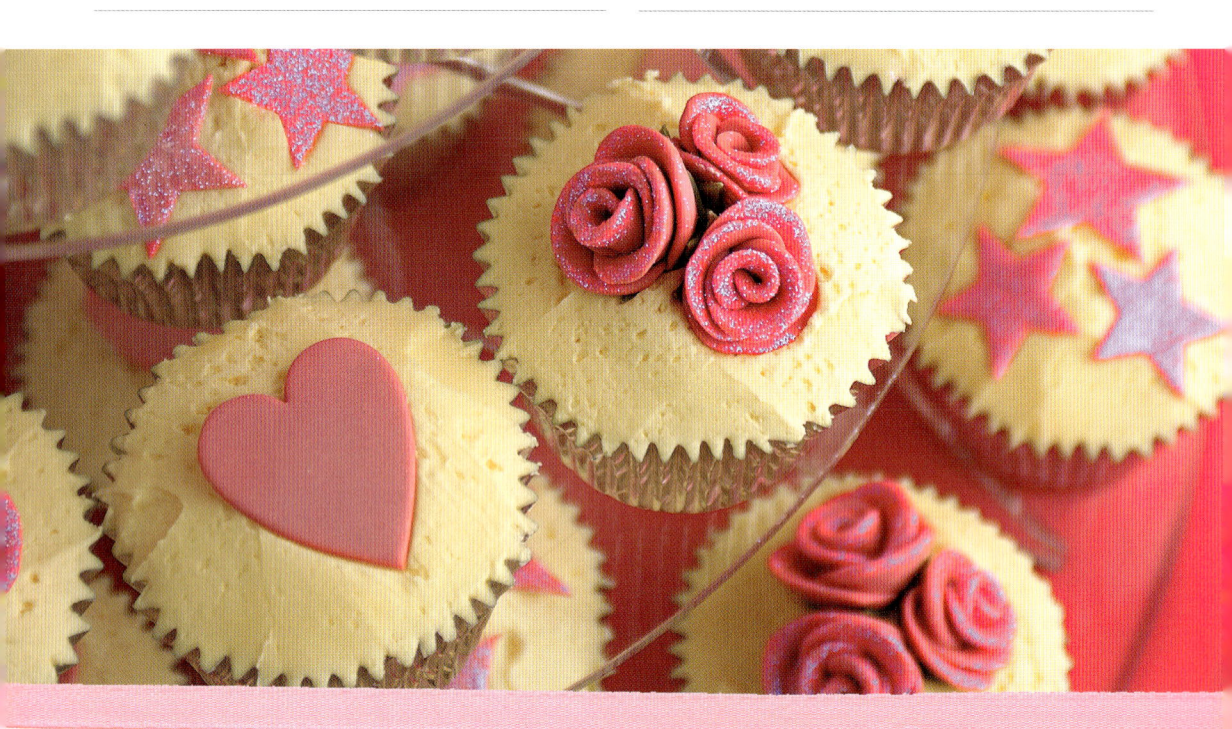

Monday 4th
Spring Bank Holiday

Tuesday 5th
Diamond Jubilee Holiday

June

Wednesday 6th

Thursday 7th

Friday 8th

Saturday 9th

Sunday 10th

June 2012

m	t	w	t	f	s	s
28	29	30	31	1	2	3
4	5	6	7	8	9	10
11	12	13	14	15	16	17
18	19	20	21	22	23	24
25	26	27	28	29	30	1
2	3	4	5	6	7	8

June

Monday 11th

Tuesday 12th

Chocolate ganache
Makes enough to cover 12 cupcakes

you will need

dark chocolate ganache:
- 200g/7oz dark chocolate
- 200ml/7 fl oz cream

white chocolate:
- 600g/1lb 5oz white chocolate
- 80ml/2¾ fl oz cream

1 Melt the chocolate and cream together in a bowl over a saucepan of gently simmering water, stirring occasionally to combine. Alternatively, use a microwave on low power, stirring thoroughly every 20 seconds or so. Be careful, however, as the chocolate can burn quickly and easily in the microwave!

2 The ganache can be used warm once it has thickened slightly and is of a pouring consistency, or it can be left to cool so that it can be spread with a palette knife. Alternatively, once completely cool it can be whisked to give a lighter texture.

June

Wednesday 13th

Thursday 14th
Flag Day (USA)

Friday 15th

Saturday 16th

Sunday 17th
Father's Day

June 2012

M	T	W	T	F	S	S
28	29	30	31	1	2	3
4	5	6	7	8	9	10
11	12	13	14	15	16	17
18	19	20	21	22	23	24
25	26	27	28	29	30	1
2	3	4	5	6	7	8

June

Monday 18th

Tuesday 19th

June

Wednesday 20th

Thursday 21st

Friday 22nd

Saturday 23rd

Sunday 24th

June 2012

M	T	W	T	F	S	S
28	29	30	31	1	2	3
4	5	6	7	8	9	10
11	12	13	14	15	16	17
18	19	20	21	22	23	24
25	26	27	28	29	30	1
2	3	4	5	6	7	8

June–July

Monday 25th

Tuesday 26th

June–July

Wednesday 27th

Thursday 28th

Friday 29th

Saturday 30th

Sunday 1st

June 2012						
m	t	w	t	f	s	s
28	29	30	31	1	2	3
4	5	6	7	8	9	10
11	12	13	14	15	16	17
18	19	20	21	22	23	24
25	26	27	28	29	30	1
2	3	4	5	6	7	8

› July

Monday 2nd

Tuesday 3rd

Wednesday 4th
Independence Day (USA)

July

Saturday 7th

Thursday 5th

Sunday 8th

Friday 6th

July 2012

m	t	w	t	f	s	s
25	26	27	28	29	30	1
2	3	4	5	6	7	8
9	10	11	12	13	14	15
16	17	18	19	20	21	22
23	24	25	26	27	28	29
30	31	1	2	3	4	5

July

Monday 9th

Tuesday 10th

July

Wednesday 11th

Thursday 12th

Friday 13th

Saturday 14th

Sunday 15th

July 2012

M	T	W	T	F	S	S
25	26	27	28	29	30	1
2	3	4	5	6	7	8
9	10	11	12	13	14	15
16	17	18	19	20	21	22
23	24	25	26	27	28	29
30	31	1	2	3	4	5

July

Monday 16th

Tuesday 17th

Buttercream — Makes enough to cover 12 cupcakes

you will need
- 100g/3½oz slightly salted butter, softened
- 200g/7oz icing (confectioners') sugar
- 1 tbsp/15ml water
- 1 tsp/5ml vanilla extract or alternative flavouring (see below)

1 Put the butter and icing (confectioners') sugar in the bowl of an electric mixer and mix together, starting on a low speed to prevent the mixture from going everywhere.

2 Add the water and vanilla extract or other flavouring and increase the speed, beating the buttercream really well until it becomes pale, light and fluffy.

3 Store the buttercream for up to two weeks in the refrigerator in an airtight container.

flavour variations
- **citrus** add the finely grated zest of one lemon or orange
- **chocolate** stir in 90g (3¼oz) melted white, milk or dark (semisweet or bittersweet) chocolate
- **passion fruit** stir in 1 tsp/5ml strained and reduced passion fruit pulp
- **coffee** add 1 tsp/5ml coffee extract
- **almond** add a few drops of almond extract

July

Wednesday 18th

Thursday 19th

Friday 20th

Saturday 21st

Sunday 22nd

July 2012

m	t	w	t	f	s	s
25	26	27	28	29	30	1
2	3	4	5	6	7	8
9	10	11	12	13	14	15
16	17	18	19	20	21	22
23	24	25	26	27	28	29
30	31	1	2	3	4	5

July

Monday 23rd

Tuesday 24th

Wednesday 25th

July

Thursday 26th

Sunday 29th

Friday 27th

Saturday 28th

July 2012

m	t	w	t	f	s	s
25	26	27	28	29	30	1
2	3	4	5	6	7	8
9	10	11	12	13	14	15
16	17	18	19	20	21	22
23	24	25	26	27	28	29
30	31	1	2	3	4	5

July–August

Monday 30th

Tuesday 31st

Wednesday 1st

July–August

Saturday 4th

Thursday 2nd

Sunday 5th

Friday 3rd

August 2012

m	t	w	t	f	s	s
30	31	1	2	3	4	5
6	7	8	9	10	11	12
13	14	15	16	17	18	19
20	21	22	23	24	25	26
27	28	29	30	31	1	2
3	4	5	6	7	8	9

August

Monday 6th

Tuesday 7th

August

Wednesday 8th

Thursday 9th

Friday 10th

Saturday 11th

Sunday 12th

August 2012

m	t	w	t	f	s	s
30	31	1	2	3	4	5
6	7	8	9	10	11	12
13	14	15	16	17	18	19
20	21	22	23	24	25	26
27	28	29	30	31	1	2
3	4	5	6	7	8	9

August

Monday 13th

Tuesday 14th

Wednesday 15th

August

Saturday 18th

Thursday 16th

Sunday 19th

Friday 17th

August 2012

M	T	W	T	F	S	S
30	31	1	2	3	4	5
6	7	8	9	10	11	12
13	14	15	16	17	18	19
20	21	22	23	24	25	26
27	28	29	30	31	1	2
3	4	5	6	7	8	9

August

Monday 20th

Tuesday 21st

Wednesday 22nd

August

Thursday 23rd

Friday 24th

Saturday 25th

Sunday 26th

August 2012

m	t	w	t	f	s	s
30	31	1	2	3	4	5
6	7	8	9	10	11	12
13	14	15	16	17	18	19
20	21	22	23	24	25	26
27	28	29	30	31	1	2
3	4	5	6	7	8	9

August–September

Monday 27th
Summer Bank Holiday

Tuesday 28th

August–September

Wednesday 29th

Thursday 30th

Friday 31st

Saturday 1st

Sunday 2nd

August 2012

M	T	W	T	F	S	S
30	31	1	2	3	4	5
6	7	8	9	10	11	12
13	14	15	16	17	18	19
20	21	22	23	24	25	26
27	28	29	30	31	1	2
3	4	5	6	7	8	9

September

Monday 3rd
Labor Day (USA)

Tuesday 4th

Honey cake — Makes 24 cupcakes

you will need

- 225g/8oz unsalted (sweet) butter
- 250g/9oz clear honey (the better the quality, the better the flavour!)
- 100g/3½oz soft light brown sugar
- 3 large eggs, beaten
- 300g/10oz self-raising (self-rising) flour, sifted

1 Preheat the oven to 160°C/320°F/Gas 3.

2 Line the cupcake tins with cupcake cases.

3 Place the butter, honey and sugar into a saucepan and warm over a low heat until the sugar has dissolved and the butter melted. Boil the mixture for one minute, then allow to cool and thicken.

4 Beat the eggs into the cooled mixture.

5 Place the flour into a bowl, then beat in the honey mixture until you have a smooth batter.

6 Spoon or pour the mixture into the cupcake cases so that they are about two-thirds full.

7 Bake for about 25 minutes, or until a fine skewer inserted into the centre of one of the cupcakes comes out clean.

8 Allow to cool in the tray for 5 minutes before removing to a wire rack.

9 Warm 2 tbsp/30ml of honey in a small pan and brush over the tops of the cakes to glaze. Allow to cool completely.

September

Wednesday 5th

Saturday 8th

Thursday 6th

Sunday 9th

Friday 7th

September 2012

M	T	W	T	F	S	S
26	27	28	29	30	1	2
3	4	5	6	7	8	9
10	11	12	13	14	15	16
17	18	19	20	21	22	23
24	25	26	27	28	29	30
1	2	3	4	5	6	7

September

Monday 10th

Tuesday 11th

Wednesday 12th

September

Saturday 15th

Thursday 13th

Sunday 16th

Friday 14th

September 2012

M	T	W	T	F	S	S
26	27	28	29	30	1	2
3	4	5	6	7	8	9
10	11	12	13	14	15	16
17	18	19	20	21	22	23
24	25	26	27	28	29	30
1	2	3	4	5	6	7

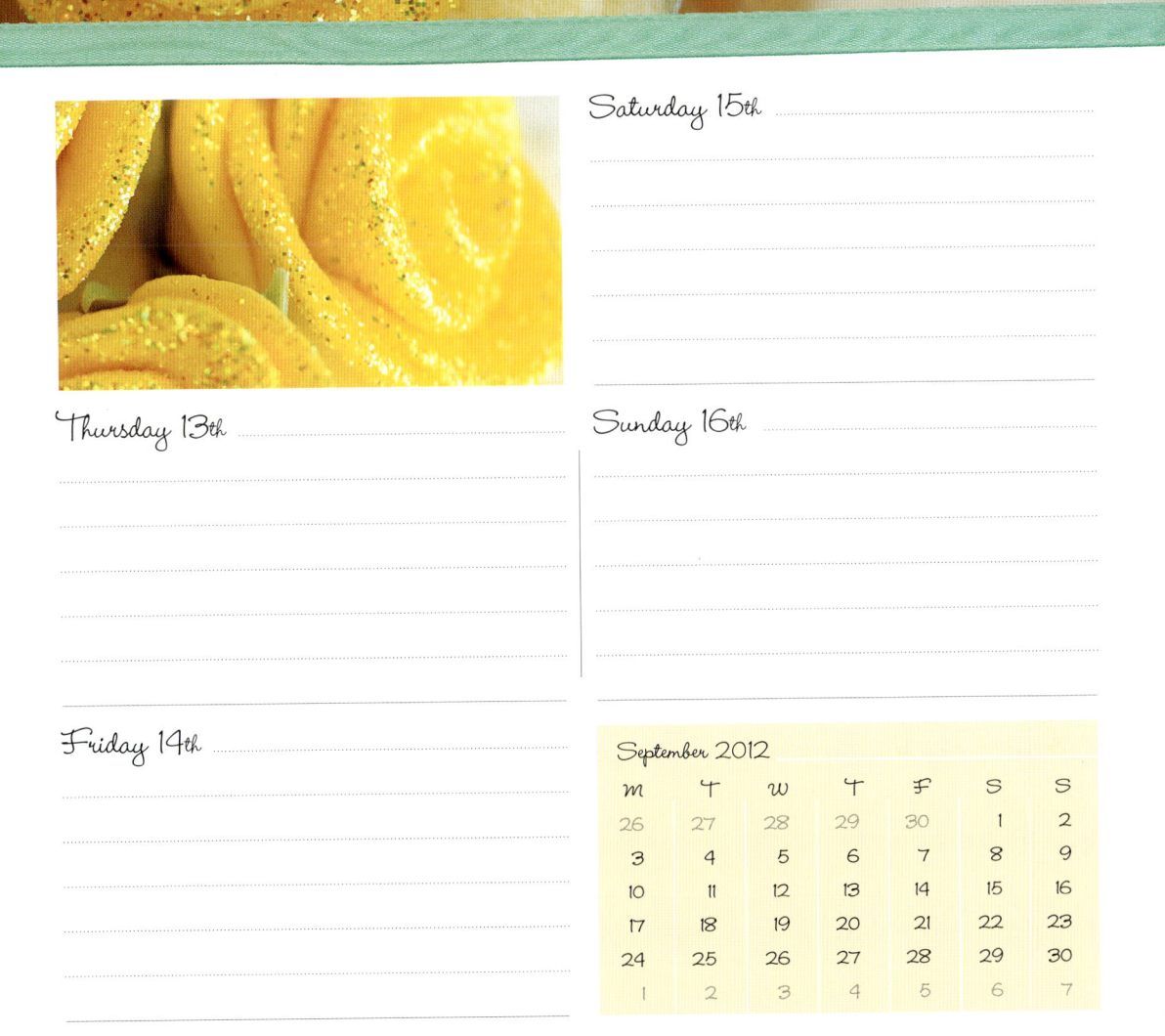

September

Monday 17th

Tuesday 18th

September

Wednesday 19th

Thursday 20th

Friday 21st

Saturday 22nd

Sunday 23rd

September 2012

M	T	W	T	F	S	S
26	27	28	29	30	1	2
3	4	5	6	7	8	9
10	11	12	13	14	15	16
17	18	19	20	21	22	23
24	25	26	27	28	29	30
1	2	3	4	5	6	7

September

Monday 24th

Tuesday 25th

September

Wednesday 26th

Thursday 27th

Friday 28th

Saturday 29th

Sunday 30th

September 2012

M	T	W	T	F	S	S
26	27	28	29	30	1	2
3	4	5	6	7	8	9
10	11	12	13	14	15	16
17	18	19	20	21	22	23
24	25	26	27	28	29	30
1	2	3	4	5	6	7

October

Monday 1st

Tuesday 2nd

Wednesday 3rd

October

Thursday 4th

Friday 5th

Saturday 6th

Sunday 7th

October 2012

m	t	w	t	f	s	s
1	2	3	4	5	6	7
8	9	10	11	12	13	14
15	16	17	18	19	20	21
22	23	24	25	26	27	28
29	30	31	1	2	3	4
5	6	7	8	9	10	11

October

Monday 8th
Columbus Day (USA)

Tuesday 9th

October

Wednesday 10th

Thursday 11th

Friday 12th

Saturday 13th

Sunday 14th

October 2012

M	T	W	T	F	S	S
1	2	3	4	5	6	7
8	9	10	11	12	13	14
15	16	17	18	19	20	21
22	23	24	25	26	27	28
29	30	31	1	2	3	4
5	6	7	8	9	10	11

October

Monday 15th

Tuesday 16th

October

Wednesday 17th

Thursday 18th

Friday 19th

Saturday 20th

Sunday 21st

October 2012

M	T	W	T	F	S	S
1	2	3	4	5	6	7
8	9	10	11	12	13	14
15	16	17	18	19	20	21
22	23	24	25	26	27	28
29	30	31	1	2	3	4
5	6	7	8	9	10	11

October

Monday 22nd

Tuesday 23rd

Wednesday 24th

October

Saturday 27th

Thursday 25th

Sunday 28th
British Summertime (BST) ends

Friday 26th

October 2012

m	t	w	t	f	s	s
1	2	3	4	5	6	7
8	9	10	11	12	13	14
15	16	17	18	19	20	21
22	23	24	25	26	27	28
29	30	31	1	2	3	4
5	6	7	8	9	10	11

October–November

Monday 29th

Tuesday 30th

October–November

Wednesday 31st
Halloween

Thursday 1st
All Saints Day

Friday 2nd

Saturday 3rd

Sunday 4th

November 2012

M	T	W	T	F	S	S
29	30	31	1	2	3	4
5	6	7	8	9	10	11
12	13	14	15	16	17	18
19	20	21	22	23	24	25
26	27	28	29	30	1	2
3	4	5	6	7	8	9

November

Monday 5th
Guy Fawkes Night

Tuesday 6th

November

Wednesday 7th

Saturday 10th

Thursday 8th

Sunday 11th
Remembrance Day

Friday 9th

November 2012						
m	t	w	t	f	s	s
29	30	31	1	2	3	4
5	6	7	8	9	10	11
12	13	14	15	16	17	18
19	20	21	22	23	24	25
26	27	28	29	30	1	2
3	4	5	6	7	8	9

November

Monday 12th
Veterans' Day (USA)

Tuesday 13th

Wednesday 14th

November

Saturday 17th

Thursday 15th

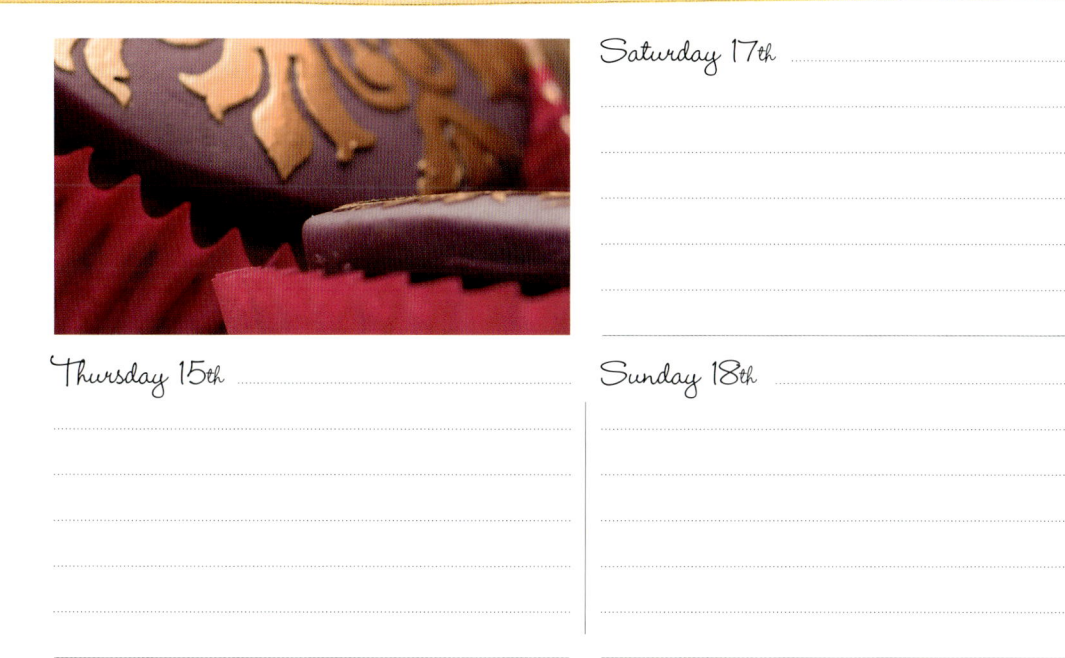

Sunday 18th

Friday 16th

November 2012

M	T	W	T	F	S	S
29	30	31	1	2	3	4
5	6	7	8	9	10	11
12	13	14	15	16	17	18
19	20	21	22	23	24	25
26	27	28	29	30	1	2
3	4	5	6	7	8	9

November

Monday 19th

Tuesday 20th

Banana and spice Makes 12 cupcakes

you will need
- 150g/5½oz unsalted (sweet) butter, softened
- 150g/5½oz light or dark brown sugar
- 3 medium eggs
- 150g/5½oz self-raising (self-rising) flour
- ½ tsp mixed spice (apple pie spice)
- 1 large over-ripe banana

1 Preheat the oven to 170°C/325°F/Gas 3.

2 Line the cupcake tin with cupcake cases.

3 In a large electric mixer, beat the butter and sugar together until light and fluffy.

4 Add the eggs gradually, beating well between each addition.

5 Sift the flour with the spice and add to the mixture. Mix very carefully until just combined.

6 Remove the mixing bowl from the mixer, mash the banana and fold it through the mixture gently with a spatula.

7 Evenly spoon or pipe the mixture into the cases and bake in the oven for approximately 20 minutes or until a skewer inserted into the centre of one of the cupcakes comes out clean.

8 Allow the cakes to cool in the tin for 10 minutes before removing to a wire rack to cool completely.

November

Wednesday 21st

Saturday 24th

Thursday 22nd
Thanksgiving Day (USA)

Sunday 25th

Friday 23rd

November 2012

m	t	w	t	f	s	s
29	30	31	1	2	3	4
5	6	7	8	9	10	11
12	13	14	15	16	17	18
19	20	21	22	23	24	25
26	27	28	29	30	1	2
3	4	5	6	7	8	9

November–December

Monday 26th

Tuesday 27th

November–December

Wednesday 28th

Thursday 29th

Friday 30th
St Andrew's Day

Saturday 1st

Sunday 2nd

November 2012

M	T	W	T	F	S	S
29	30	31	1	2	3	4
5	6	7	8	9	10	11
12	13	14	15	16	17	18
19	20	21	22	23	24	25
26	27	28	29	30	1	2
3	4	5	6	7	8	9

December

Monday 3rd

Tuesday 4th

Wednesday 5th

December

Saturday 8th

Thursday 6th

Sunday 9th

Friday 7th

December 2012						
m	t	w	t	f	s	s
26	27	28	29	30	1	2
3	4	5	6	7	8	9
10	11	12	13	14	15	16
17	18	19	20	21	22	23
24	25	26	27	28	29	30
31	1	2	3	4	5	6

December

Monday 10th

Tuesday 11th

December

Wednesday 12th

Thursday 13th

Friday 14th

Saturday 15th

Sunday 16th

December 2012

m	t	w	t	f	s	s
26	27	28	29	30	1	2
3	4	5	6	7	8	9
10	11	12	13	14	15	16
17	18	19	20	21	22	23
24	25	26	27	28	29	30
31	1	2	3	4	5	6

December

Monday 17th

Tuesday 18th

Wednesday 19th

December

Saturday 22nd

Thursday 20th

Sunday 23rd

Friday 21st

December 2012

m	t	w	t	f	s	s
26	27	28	29	30	1	2
3	4	5	6	7	8	9
10	11	12	13	14	15	16
17	18	19	20	21	22	23
24	25	26	27	28	29	30
31	1	2	3	4	5	6

December

Monday 24th

Tuesday 25th
Christmas Day

Wednesday 26th
Boxing Day

December

Saturday 29th

Thursday 27th

Sunday 30th

Friday 28th

December 2012						
m	t	w	t	f	s	s
26	27	28	29	30	1	2
3	4	5	6	7	8	9
10	11	12	13	14	15	16
17	18	19	20	21	22	23
24	25	26	27	28	29	30
31	1	2	3	4	5	6

December–January

Monday 31st
New Year's Eve

Tuesday 1st
New Year's Day

Wednesday 2nd

December–January

Saturday 5th

Thursday 3rd

Sunday 6th

Friday 4th

January 2013

m	t	w	t	f	s	s
31	1	2	3	4	5	6
7	8	9	10	11	12	13
14	15	16	17	18	19	20
21	22	23	24	25	26	27
28	29	30	31	1	2	3
4	5	6	7	8	9	10

2012

January 2012
m	t	w	t	f	s	s
26	27	28	29	30	31	1
2	3	4	5	6	7	8
9	10	11	12	13	14	15
16	17	18	19	20	21	22
23	24	25	26	27	28	29
30	31	1	2	3	4	5

February 2012
m	t	w	t	f	s	s
30	31	1	2	3	4	5
6	7	8	9	10	11	12
13	14	15	16	17	18	19
20	21	22	23	24	25	26
27	28	29	1	2	3	4
5	6	7	8	9	10	11

March 2012
m	t	w	t	f	s	s
27	28	29	1	2	3	4
5	6	7	8	9	10	11
12	13	14	15	16	17	18
19	20	21	22	23	24	25
26	27	28	29	30	31	1
2	3	4	5	6	7	8

April 2012
m	t	w	t	f	s	s
26	27	28	29	30	31	1
2	3	4	5	6	7	8
9	10	11	12	13	14	15
16	17	18	19	20	21	22
23	24	25	26	27	28	29
30	1	2	3	4	5	6

May 2012
m	t	w	t	f	s	s
30	1	2	3	4	5	6
7	8	9	10	11	12	13
14	15	16	17	18	19	20
21	22	23	24	25	26	27
28	29	30	31	1	2	3
4	5	6	7	8	9	10

June 2012
m	t	w	t	f	s	s
28	29	30	31	1	2	3
4	5	6	7	8	9	10
11	12	13	14	15	16	17
18	19	20	21	22	23	24
25	26	27	28	29	30	1
2	3	4	5	6	7	8

2012

July 2012

m	t	w	t	f	s	s
25	26	27	28	29	30	1
2	3	4	5	6	7	8
9	10	11	12	13	14	15
16	17	18	19	20	21	22
23	24	25	26	27	28	29
30	31	1	2	3	4	5

October 2012

m	t	w	t	f	s	s
1	2	3	4	5	6	7
8	9	10	11	12	13	14
15	16	17	18	19	20	21
22	23	24	25	26	27	28
29	30	31	1	2	3	4
5	6	7	8	9	10	11

August 2012

m	t	w	t	f	s	s
30	31	1	2	3	4	5
6	7	8	9	10	11	12
13	14	15	16	17	18	19
20	21	22	23	24	25	26
27	28	29	30	31	1	2
3	4	5	6	7	8	9

November 2012

m	t	w	t	f	s	s
29	30	31	1	2	3	4
5	6	7	8	9	10	11
12	13	14	15	16	17	18
19	20	21	22	23	24	25
26	27	28	29	30	1	2
3	4	5	6	7	8	9

September 2012

m	t	w	t	f	s	s
27	28	29	30	31	1	2
3	4	5	6	7	8	9
10	11	12	13	14	15	16
17	18	19	20	21	22	23
24	25	26	27	28	29	30
1	2	3	4	5	6	7

December 2012

m	t	w	t	f	s	s
26	27	28	29	30	1	2
3	4	5	6	7	8	9
10	11	12	13	14	15	16
17	18	19	20	21	22	23
24	25	26	27	28	29	30
31	1	2	3	4	5	6

2011

2011 ...the baking year passed...

January

m	t	w	t	f	s	s
27	28	29	30	31	1	2
3	4	5	6	7	8	9
10	11	12	13	14	15	16
17	18	19	20	21	22	23
24	25	26	27	28	29	30
31	1	2	3	4	5	6

February

m	t	w	t	f	s	s
24	25	26	27	28	29	30
31	1	2	3	4	5	6
7	8	9	10	11	12	13
14	15	16	17	18	19	20
21	22	23	24	25	26	27
28	1	2	3	4	5	6

March

m	t	w	t	f	s	s
28	1	2	3	4	5	6
7	8	9	10	11	12	13
14	15	16	17	18	19	20
21	22	23	24	25	26	27
28	29	30	31	1	2	3
4	5	6	7	8	9	10

April

m	t	w	t	f	s	s
28	29	30	31	1	2	3
4	5	6	7	8	9	10
11	12	13	14	15	16	17
18	19	20	21	22	23	24
25	26	27	28	29	30	1
2	3	4	5	6	7	8

May

m	t	w	t	f	s	s
25	26	27	28	29	30	1
2	3	4	5	6	7	8
9	10	11	12	13	14	15
16	17	18	19	20	21	22
23	24	25	26	27	28	29
30	31	1	2	3	4	5

June

m	t	w	t	f	s	s
30	31	1	2	3	4	5
6	7	8	9	10	11	12
13	14	15	16	17	18	19
20	21	22	23	24	25	26
27	28	29	30	1	2	3
4	5	6	7	8	9	10

July

m	t	w	t	f	s	s
27	28	29	30	1	2	3
4	5	6	7	8	9	10
11	12	13	14	15	16	17
18	19	20	21	22	23	24
25	26	27	28	29	30	31
1	2	3	4	5	6	7

August

m	t	w	t	f	s	s
25	26	27	28	29	30	31
1	2	3	4	5	6	7
8	9	10	11	12	13	14
15	16	17	18	19	20	21
22	23	24	25	26	27	28
29	30	31	1	2	3	4

September

m	t	w	t	f	s	s
29	30	31	1	2	3	4
5	6	7	8	9	10	11
12	13	14	15	16	17	18
19	20	21	22	23	24	25
26	27	28	29	30	1	2
3	4	5	6	7	8	9

October

m	t	w	t	f	s	s
26	27	28	29	30	1	2
3	4	5	6	7	8	9
10	11	12	13	14	15	16
17	18	19	20	21	22	23
24	25	26	27	28	29	30
31	1	2	3	4	5	6

November

m	t	w	t	f	s	s
24	25	26	27	28	29	30
31	1	2	3	4	5	6
7	8	9	10	11	12	13
14	15	16	17	18	19	20
21	22	23	24	25	26	27
28	29	30	1	2	3	4

December

m	t	w	t	f	s	s
28	29	30	1	2	3	4
5	6	7	8	9	10	11
12	13	14	15	16	17	18
19	20	21	22	23	24	25
26	27	28	29	30	31	1
2	3	4	5	6	7	8

2013

2013 ...the baking year ahead...

January
m	t	w	t	f	s	s
24	25	26	27	28	29	30
31	1	2	3	4	5	6
7	8	9	10	11	12	13
14	15	16	17	18	19	20
21	22	23	24	25	26	27
28	29	30	31	1	2	3

February
m	t	w	t	f	s	s
28	29	30	31	1	2	3
4	5	6	7	8	9	10
11	12	13	14	15	16	17
18	19	20	21	22	23	24
25	26	27	28	1	2	3
4	5	6	7	8	9	10

March
m	t	w	t	f	s	s
25	26	27	28	1	2	3
4	5	6	7	8	9	10
11	12	13	14	15	16	17
18	19	20	21	22	23	24
25	26	27	28	29	30	31
1	2	3	4	5	6	7

April
m	t	w	t	f	s	s
25	26	27	28	29	30	31
1	2	3	4	5	6	7
8	9	10	11	12	13	14
15	16	17	18	19	20	21
22	23	24	25	26	27	28
29	30	1	2	3	4	5

May
m	t	w	t	f	s	s
29	30	1	2	3	4	5
6	7	8	9	10	11	12
13	14	15	16	17	18	19
20	21	22	23	24	25	26
27	28	29	30	31	1	2
3	4	5	6	7	8	9

June
m	t	w	t	f	s	s
27	28	29	30	31	1	2
3	4	5	6	7	8	9
10	11	12	13	14	15	16
17	18	19	20	21	22	23
24	25	26	27	28	29	30
1	2	3	4	5	6	7

July
m	t	w	t	f	s	s
24	25	26	27	28	29	30
1	2	3	4	5	6	7
8	9	10	11	12	13	14
15	16	17	18	19	20	21
22	23	24	25	26	27	28
29	30	31	1	2	3	4

August
m	t	w	t	f	s	s
29	30	31	1	2	3	4
5	6	7	8	9	10	11
12	13	14	15	16	17	18
19	20	21	22	23	24	25
26	27	28	29	30	31	1
2	3	4	5	6	7	8

September
m	t	w	t	f	s	s
26	27	28	29	30	31	1
2	3	4	5	6	7	8
9	10	11	12	13	14	15
16	17	18	19	20	21	22
23	24	25	26	27	28	29
30	1	2	3	4	5	6

October
m	t	w	t	f	s	s
23	24	25	26	27	28	29
30	1	2	3	4	5	6
7	8	9	10	11	12	13
14	15	16	17	18	19	20
21	22	23	24	25	26	27
28	29	30	31	1	2	3

November
m	t	w	t	f	s	s
28	29	30	31	1	2	3
4	5	6	7	8	9	10
11	12	13	14	15	16	17
18	19	20	21	22	23	24
25	26	27	28	29	30	1
2	3	4	5	6	7	8

December
m	t	w	t	f	s	s
25	26	27	28	29	30	1
2	3	4	5	6	7	8
9	10	11	12	13	14	15
16	17	18	19	20	21	22
23	24	25	26	27	28	29
30	31	1	2	3	4	5

bake me I'm yours — books

The images included in the Bake Me I'm Yours... Cupcake Diary 2012 have all been selected from the great range of sugarcraft books published by David & Charles. If you would like to find out more about any of the cupcakes featured, why not treat yourself to a few of these inspiring books. For more information visit: www.bakeme.com.

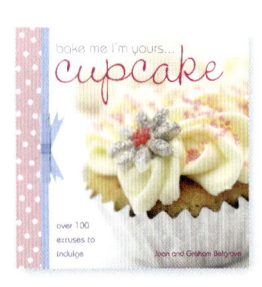

Bake Me I'm Yours... Cupcake
ISBN-13: 978-0-7153-3762-2

Over 100 ways to bake, frost, decorate, display and indulge! Treat yourself to a piece of cupcake heaven with divine designs that are devilishly simple.

Bake Me I'm Yours... Cookie
ISBN-13: 978-0-7153-3763-9

Bake delicious cookies in all shapes and sizes using simple but effective techniques. Create your own designs, from cute teddy bears to gorgeous flowers and chic handbags.

Bake Me I'm Yours... Chocolate
ISBN-13: 978-0-7153-3764-6

Treat everyone with over 25 heavenly chocolate creations, including cakes, truffles and brownies. Learn how to temper chocolate and create stunning decorations.

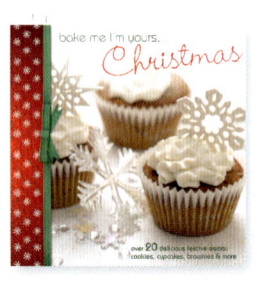

Bake Me I'm Yours... Christmas
ISBN-13: 978-0-7153-3639-7

A festive collection of over 20 tempting projects, which give the perfect excuse to bake at Christmas. With ideas for edible decorations and gifts that will delight your guests!

bake me I'm yours – books

Bake Me I'm Yours... Collection

ISBN-13: 978-0-7153-3639-7

Discover over 200 ways to enjoy sweet treats. Create cupcakes, cookies and chocolate goodies as great gifts for friends, fabulous food for parties or indulgences just for you! With easy-to-follow instructions, every delicious bite is simple to make and fun to decorate.

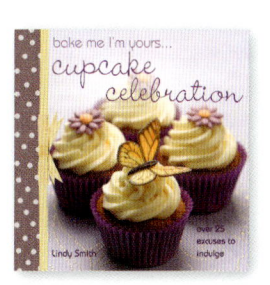

Bake Me I'm Yours... Cupcake Celebration

ISBN-13: 978-0-7153-3770-7

Celebrate in style, with over 25 irresistible cupcake ideas. Add that special touch to every occasion following the beautiful designs and delicious recipes.

Bake Me I'm Yours... Cupcake Love

ISBN-13: 978-0-7153-3781-3

An indulgent collection of cupcake projects, recipes and ideas for every romantic occasion. Tempt loved ones with the 20 gorgeous designs.

Bake Me I'm Yours... Whoopie Pies

PUBLISHING IN AUGUST 2011

ISBN-13: 978-1-4463-0068-8

Over 70 great excuses to bake, fill and decorate these tempting treats! Includes everything you need to create stunning whoopie pies for your special occasions.

Bake Me I'm Yours... Cake Pops

PUBLISHING IN SEPTEMBER 2011

ISBN-13: 978-1-4463-0137-1

Over 30 colourful projects, from cute animals and romantic wedding rings, to creepy Halloween creatures and festive Christmas characters.

the books

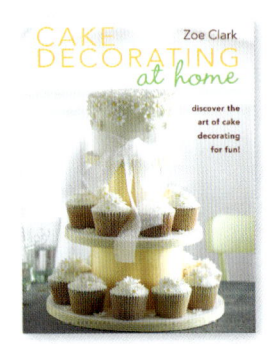

Cake Decorating at Home

ISBN-13: 978-0-7153-3758-5

A delicious collection of 30 homemade treats to delight your friends and family all year round. Packed with recipes and designs for cakes, cupcakes, mini cakes, fondant fancies and cookies.

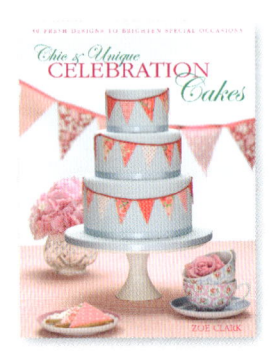

Chic & Unique Celebration Cakes

ISBN-13: 978-0-7153-3838-4

Create gorgeous celebration cakes that are as colourful and special as the occasion. The delicious designs extend to cupcakes, mini cakes, fondant fancies, cookies and truffles.

Sweet & Simple Party Cakes

ISBN-13: 978-0-7153-2687-9

Create a sweet sensation for any occasion with over 40 elegant and contemporary cake designs. Adorable cupcakes and mini cakes offer an appealing alternative or addition.

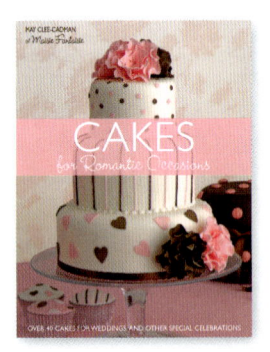

Cakes for Romantic Occasions

ISBN-13: 978-0-7153-3154-5

Over 40 stunning designs for cakes, cupcakes and cookies. Create stylish confections for every romantic occasion, whether it's a wedding cake, anniversary cupcakes or Valentine's Day cookies.

the books

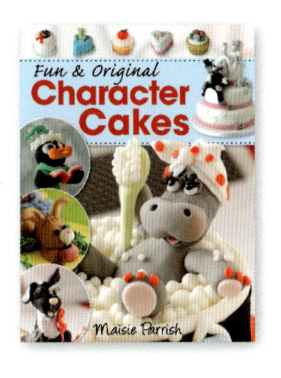

Fun & Original Character Cakes

ISBN-13: 978-0-7153-3005-0

Learn how to create unique sugarpaste characters with simple step-by-step instructions from expert Maisie Parrish. All of the cake designs are accompanied by cupcake and mini cake variations.

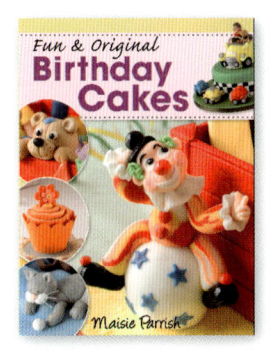

Fun & Original Birthday Cakes

ISBN-13: 978-0-7153-3833-9

Be amused and amazed by this incredible collection of brilliant birthday cakes. Add a personal touch to your celebrations with over 30 unique characters, decorations and toppers to delight loved ones.

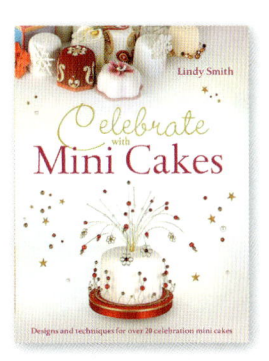

Celebrate with Mini Cakes

ISBN-13: 978-0-7153-3783-7

Features designs and techniques for over 20 celebration mini cakes. Create delicious treats for every occasion, from birthdays and children's parties to weddings and Christmas.

The Contemporary Cake Decorating Bible

PUBLISHING IN OCTOBER 2011

ISBN-13: 978-0-7153-3836-0

The ultimate guide to cake decorating techniques, from best-selling author Lindy Smith. Covers every must-know technique for all abilities and features designs for cakes, cupcakes and cookies.

the authors

Zoe Clark

Zoe's intricate work is regularly featured in national bridal magazines and she has made several apearances on wedding shows on TV. Following her success, Zoe has recently opened a new boutique in Wimbledon, London called The Cake Parlour.

www.zoeclarkcakes.com
www.thecakeparlour.com

Lindy Smith

Lindy is a talented cake designer, who teaches all around the world. She has appeared on numerous TV shows and presented a sugarcraft series on Good Food Live. She heads Lindy's Cakes Ltd, running her online shop and workshops.

www.lindyscakes.co.uk

Joan & Graham Belgrove

Joan and Graham launched The Little Cupcake Company Ltd in 2006 in response to the growing demand for celebration cupcakes. They now have an established internet business supplying unique cupcakes to both private customers and major comanies.

www.thelittlecupcakecompany.co.uk

May Clee-Cadman

May founded Maisie Fantaisie in 2003 to create unique wedding and celebration cakes. She studied Art and Design History and went on to train as a cake designer, incorporating her flair for design with her love of cake making.

www.maisiefantaisie.co.uk

the authors

Maisie Parrish

Maisie is completely self-taught and her cute and colourful characters have a unique style that is instantly recognizable. She is always busy travelling to teach and demonstrate her skills. She has enjoyed several TV appearances, including The Good Food Show and QVC.

www.maisieparrish.com

Tracey Mann

Tracey owns a successful cake design business, Tracey's Cakes, and teaches classes in chocolate work. Her designs are regularly featured in cake decorating and wedding magazines. Her online mail order company produces its own brand of chocolate paste.

www.traceyscakes.co.uk

Natalie Saville & Jill Collins

Natalie and Jill own The Great Little Cake Company, founded in 2007. They specialise in using quality ingredients to create unique and eye-catching cakes and cupcakes. They recently produced a cake for the 'Wildlife Wedding' show, sponsored by Wedding TV.

www.thegreatlittlecakecompany.co.uk

Carolyn White

Carolyn, a former protégé of Lindy Smith, launched Cakes 4 Fun in 2001. She runs two busy shops in Putney, London with a talented team of designers, specializing in bespoke, contemporary and novelty cakes, and running popular cake decorating and sugarcraft courses.

www.cakes4fun.co.uk

Classes

Learn the art of cupcake decorating, Lindy Smith style, or try something a little different, cookies perhaps or even a carved cake. We have one day classes to suit all abilities and tastes.

Our current class schedule is published on our website:

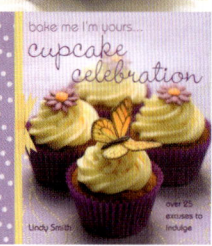

www.lindyscakes.co.uk

To create your very own stunning cupcakes visit our:

Online Shop

We offer an exquisite choice of good quality and unusual products, including:

- Colourful cupcake cases from around the world
- Super easy culinary stencils
- Designer sugarcraft cutters
- Fast & fabulous silicone moulds
- Quality essential tools
- Edible food colours in every colour of the rainbow and more

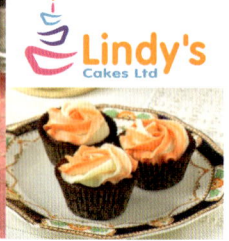

Lindy's Cakes Ltd

Alternatively call:
+44 (0)1296 622418

A DAVID & CHARLES BOOK
© F&W Media International, LTD 2011

David & Charles is an imprint of F&W Media International, LTD
Brunel House, Forde Close, Newton Abbot, TQ12 4PU, UK

F&W Media International, LTD is a subsidiary of F+W Media Inc.
4700 East Galbraith Road, Cincinnati, OH 45236, USA

First published in the UK and USA in 2011

Text, layout and photography © F&W Media International, LTD 2011

All rights reserved. No part of this publication may be reproduced, stored in a retrieval system, or transmitted, in any form or by any means, electronic or mechanical, by photocopying, recording or otherwise, without prior permission in writing from the publisher.

A catalogue record for this book is available from the British Library.

ISBN-13: 978-1-4463-0121-0 hardback
ISBN-10: 1-4463-0121-4 hardback

Printed in China by Toppan Leefung Printing Limited
for F&W Media International, LTD
Brunel House, Forde Close, Newton Abbot, TQ12 4PU, UK

The publisher would like to thank Zoe Clark and Lindy Smith for permission to include their recipes in this diary.

Recipes on pages 18, 28, 44, 64, 100 © Zoe Clark 2011
Recipes on pages 10, 54, 78 © Lindy Smith 2011

Front cover photograph by Lorna Yabsley for Bake Me I'm Yours...
Cupcake (Joan & Graham Belgrove, 2007).

Back cover photograph by Sian Irvine for Bake Me I'm Yours...
Cupcake Celebration (Lindy Smith, 2010).

F+W Media Inc. publishes high quality books on a wide range of subjects. For more great book ideas visit: www.bakeme.com

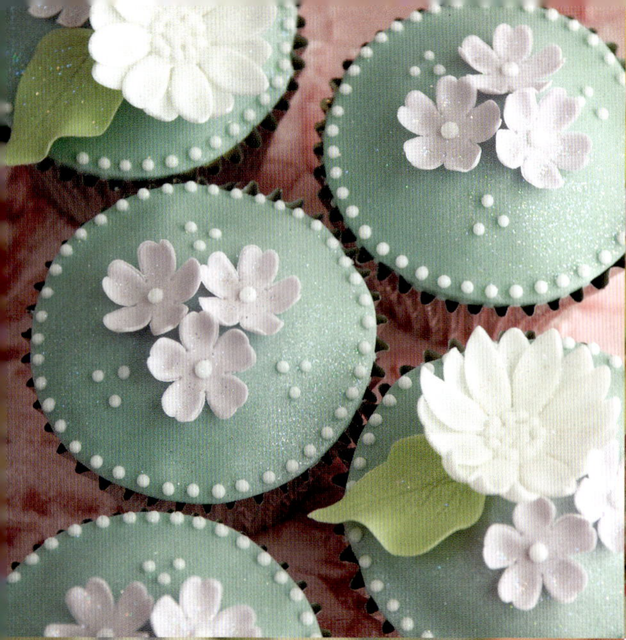
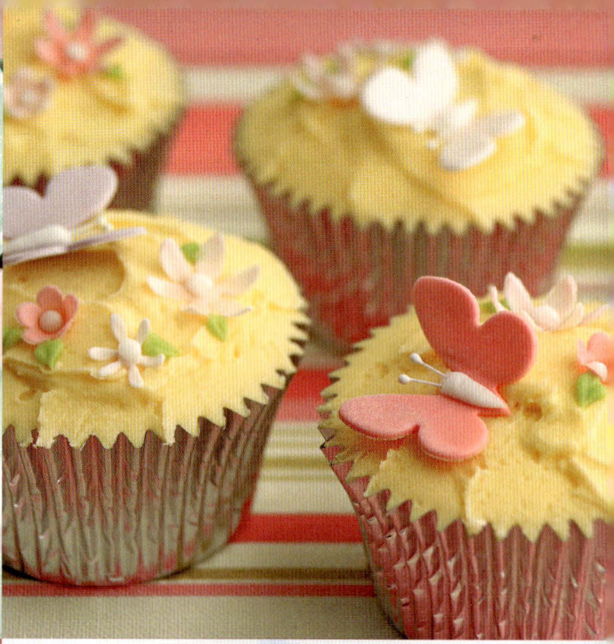
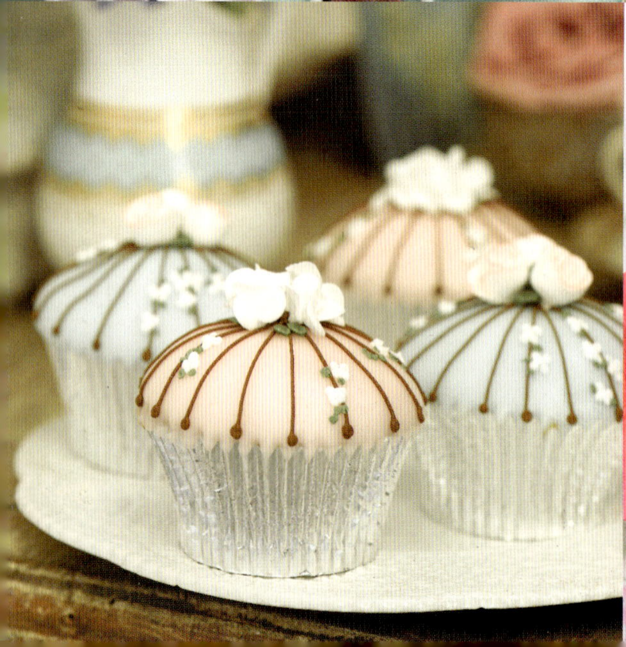
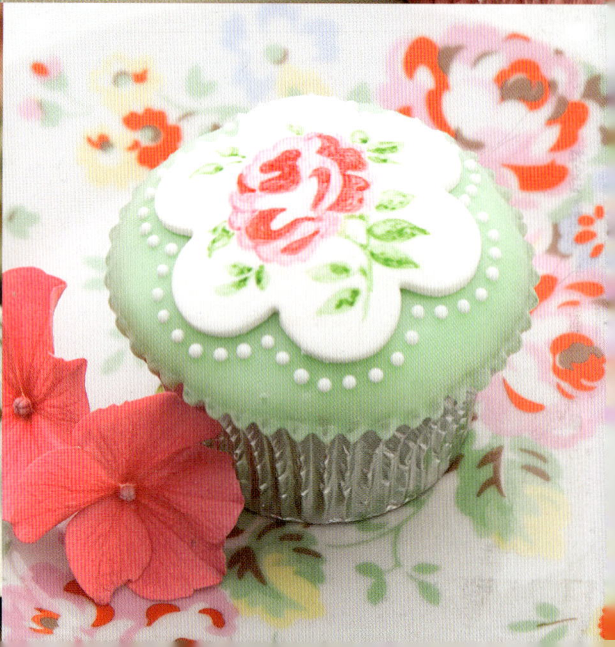